Popes
of the
Twentieth
Century

by the
Daughters of St. Paul

ST. PAUL EDITIONS

NIHIL OBSTAT:
  Rev. Richard V. Lawlor, S.J.
  Censor

IMPRIMATUR:
  ✠ Humberto Cardinal Medeiros
  Archbishop of Boston

Photo credits:
Ferdinando Paladini—cover
Felici—8, 28, 38
Giordani—56

ISBN 0-8198-5811-0 cloth
     0-8198-5812-9 paper

Printed in the U.S.A., by the Daughters of St. Paul
50 St. Paul's Ave., Boston, MA 02130

The Daughters of St. Paul are an international congregation of religious women serving the Church with the communications media.

Contents

They Called Him...
"The Master Diplomat"

Pope Leo XIII
(1878-1903)

It was the afternoon of February 20, 1878. The sky seemed to be brighter than usual. Thousands of people thronged St. Peter's Square waiting anxiously. As the white smoke rose slowly from the chimney, someone yelled: "The Pope is elected! We have a Pope!"

Slowly the window over the entrance of Saint Peter's Basilica opened. The Cardinal Deacon came forward.

"I announce to you a very great joy," he cried. "We have a Pope!"

The crowd cheered. Then he continued: "It is his most Reverend Eminence Joachim Pecci, Cardinal of the Holy Roman Church, who has taken the name *Leo XIII.*" Rome was jubilant. The name Leo XIII was on everyone's lips.

Joachim Vincent Pecci was born March 2, 1810, in a palace-like estate in the village of Carpineto, Italy. Being one of seven children of a very religious family, the boy was brought up with much love and care. His mother kept a watchful eye on this one who, as she phrased it, "danced with life."

Joachim enjoyed mountain climbing, hunting, horseback riding and hiking. A serious-minded student, he attended the Jesuit College in Viterbo. One of his classmates later wrote about him: "I can witness to the fact that while still at Viterbo, Joachim won our admiration not

11

only for his quick intelligence, but even more, for the singular purity of his life.''

Joachim majored in theology at the Gregorian University and received his doctorate. Later, he attended the Academy of Noble Ecclesiastics where he studied canon and civil law. Although unaware of it, the young man was following the course that divine Providence had laid out to prepare him for his future priestly ministry. It was not until the death of his father, in 1836, that he decided with certainty to become a priest. He was ordained in December, 1837.

In 1843, the now Monsignor Pecci was sent to Brussels as Nuncio representing the Holy Father at a time when there were many religious and political controversies. With his quick wit and graciousness, coupled with the witness of his prayer-filled life, the young Monsignor won the respect and confidence of the King and Queen. Very often when Queen Louise heard that Monsignor Pecci was on the grounds, she would hurry to gather her children and present them to him for a blessing.

Monsignor Pecci returned to Rome in 1845. Pope Gregory XVI appointed him Bishop of Perugia. There he remained for thirty-two years from 1845-1877. Bishop Pecci showed his pastoral care in various ways. Religious instruction was at the head of his concerns and the zealous prelate guided the publication of a new edition of the catechism for his diocese. He encouraged his priests to offer ongoing adult instruction as well as catechism classes for children and teenagers.

The bishop was a father to the clergy, but his most tender concern was for the seminarians. Often he would drop in, unexpected, to the seminary classrooms, and would listen from the back of the room to the lectures given to them.

The story is told of a priest-professor, late for class, who ran toward the classroom. He said a fervent prayer that today would not be one of those days when His Excellency would make an impromptu visit. As he burst into the room from the rear door, he heaved a sigh of relief at not seeing Bishop Pecci in any of the last seats. Then he rushed up to the front of the room and stopped, dumbfounded. Bishop Joachim Pecci was at the instructor's desk teaching the seminarians himself.

In 1853, Bishop Pecci was summoned by Pope Pius XI to Rome and made a Cardinal. The new Cardinal returned to his beloved Perugia and devoted himself tirelessly to his archdiocese for many more years. But in 1878, Joachim Pecci took on the burden of an area larger than Perugia, larger than his native Italy, larger even than the continent of Europe. As the "Servant of the Servants of God," Joachim Cardinal Pecci— Leo XIII—was Pope.

The twenty-five-year reign of Leo XIII covers the end of the nineteenth century and the beginning of the twentieth (1878-1903). The profound respect he soon earned from world leaders, despite the anti-clericalism and hatred of religion which was being propagated, is evident in the number of sovereigns and political powers who called on the Vicar of Christ. Even the anti-Catholic Count Bismarck of Germany manifested his admiration for the Pope by asking him to settle the disagreement between Germany and Spain over the Caroline Islands.

But it was especially in the social field that Leo XIII set the Church on a new path. In 1848, Karl Marx had issued his *Manifesto*. On May 15, 1891, Pope Leo XIII issued one of the most vital encyclicals of all time, a document which reshaped the world of labor. In *Rerum novarum, The Condition of the Working Classes,* Pope Leo said:

"Let those in charge of States make use of the provision afforded by laws and institutions; let the rich and employers be mindful of their duties; let the workers, whose cause is at stake, press their claims with reason. And since religion alone...can remove the evil, root and branch, let all reflect upon this: First and foremost, Christian morals must be re-established, without which even the weapons of prudence, which are considered especially effective, will be of no avail to secure well-being" (no. 82).

In this monumental document, the Pope spoke about labor unions and the right to strike when necessary to obtain just conditions. He advocated cooperative industries run by the workers themselves, such as farmers' cooperative dairies, and cooperative banks. He urged the formation of associations of workers to improve their social and cultural conditions.

In other words, all the benefits we take for granted today were advocated by the Pope at a time when many still thought that power, education, and money should be the possessions of only a few.

Pope Leo XIII also promoted progress in theology and philosophy, especially as presented by the genius, Thomas Aquinas.

Greatly devoted to the Blessed Mother, the Pope made her holy Rosary a most popular devotion throughout the world. Indeed, he so clearly taught her sublime role in the redemption and her privileges that we can call him a leading figure in the science of Mariology, or Marian studies.

In the field of ecumenism, too, Pope Leo's wonderful personality and keen understanding helped him establish warm relations with non-Catholic Christians.

Though rich in accomplishments, this tall, thin Pope with the perpetual smile slept little. His time was spent in prayer and in the fulfilling of his duties. His meals were frugal, consisting of black coffee for breakfast; a slice of meat, a vegetable and a piece of fruit for lunch. For supper, which was usually eaten at 10:00 p.m., the Holy Father ate an egg and a small salad. His recreation was a walk every afternoon in the Vatican Gardens.

The Pope also loved to joke. During an audience, an old gentleman said to him: "I am very happy to be permitted to see Your Holiness. Pope Pius IX also granted me an audience a few days before he died." Pope Leo replied: "If I had known that you were so dangerous to Popes, I would have postponed the audience for a few years." He loved to converse with others and had the habit of holding their hands while talking.

After a twenty-five year pontificate, the Pope fell ill with pneumonia and pleurisy. He died at the age of ninety-three, on the evening of July 20, 1903. The bells of the Eternal City rang slowly, crying for the loss of the beloved Bishop of Rome. He died, but the influence and ideas of the man who has been called the "master diplomat" live on. Such is the effect of a man of thought, of serenity and of prayer.

Twentieth-Century Sunrise

Pope St. Pius X
(1903-1914)

On August 4, 1903, a new Pope was elected to the Chair of St. Peter. This Pope of humble origins was the first Pontiff since the time of the French Revolution who did not come from the middle or upper strata of society. Until the unsuspected events of that August day, he had been called Giuseppe, or Joseph, Sarto. He took for his pontifical name that of Pius, in memory and in honor of those Pontiffs who had suffered much for the Church.

Joseph Sarto was born on June 25, 1835, in the village of Riëse, Italy, not far from Venice. His mother was a seamstress and his father a municipal messenger. He had nine brothers and sisters; his family worked hard and lived virtuously.

From a very early age, Joseph wished to become a priest. Having received a scholarship from the Patriarch of Venice, he was able to study for eight years at the seminary of Padua. Young Sarto proved to be an excellent student and finished his years of training and education with distinction. In September of 1858, he was ordained to the priesthood and was promptly assigned to the parish of Tombolo.

It didn't take long for the parishioners to realize that their new pastor was truly a blessing for them. In his own quiet, humble way, Father Sarto showed himself to be a true priest of God. He had three particular areas of concentration.

First of all, the homily at Mass was given his utmost attention: good preparation and delivery. Secondly, he made available ongoing catechetical instruction for all the members of the parish. And thirdly, he took a personal interest in the people entrusted to his care, concerning himself about their every need—spiritual and material. The poor were always at his door.

Father Sarto was then made chancellor of his diocese of Treviso, combining numerous duties with those of teacher and spiritual director of the seminary. On November 16, 1884, he became Bishop of Mantua. After episcopal ordination in Rome, he returned to his native village of Riëse to visit Mama Margherita, his mother. She grasped his hand and carefully kissed his episcopal ring. With her characteristic insight, Mama told him, "Ah, my son, remember, you would not have this fine ring if it weren't for this one." She held up her hand with its worn wedding band. Bishop Sarto then kissed his mother's ring; there were tears in his eyes.

The diocese of Mantua in the mid-1800's was in need of spiritual renewal. The new bishop decided that the best way to revitalize a flock that had been scattered mainly because of the scarcity of priests was to renew the clergy. He started with the diocesan seminary by improving the buildings and restoring discipline, both academic and spiritual. He rotated the teaching staff, placing better prepared priests in key positions. Then he visited each and every parish, one by one, as a father visits his children. When he left Mantua to become Patriarch of Venice nine years later, he left a model diocese.

The great Pope Leo XIII made Bishop Joseph Sarto a Cardinal and appointed him Patriarch of Venice. How did the Cardinal spend his nine years in Venice? As pastor of the diocese, he renewed the seminary first of all. Canon Law and Church music were areas of his concern, along with biblical studies, Church history, archaeology and social and political science. These very concerns were to accompany him to the Vatican in 1903.

Cardinal Sarto was a man of the people. He even spoke the dialect of the Venetians. He spent many an evening chatting with the folks who would gather in the famous St. Mark's Square to pass the time in those pre-television days.

One day, the Cardinal and the auxiliary bishop went to the home of a sick child to administer the Sacrament of Confirmation. On their way, they passed a woman carrying a youngster. Neither the Cardinal nor the bishop wore any external signs of their dignity; both were dressed as simple priests. Yet the little child pointed at Cardinal Sarto and announced to his mama: "Look, there is the Pope!" At that, the auxiliary bishop muttered under his breath, "...Out of the mouths of infants you have perfected praise...." And thus it came to be.

On July 20, 1903, after twenty-five years of reign, Pope Leo XIII went to his eternal reward. On July 26, Cardinal Sarto left Venice and his beloved people with the now historic words: "Alive or dead, I will return to my dear Venice which I shall never forget." He was not to return alive.

August 4, 1903, will never be forgotten in the annals of twentieth-century Church historians. The election of Cardinal Sarto as Pope was of great importance to the Church and to the world. The next eleven years would be enough to try the virtue of the most capable. With the fast-surfacing problems within the Church as well as on the world scene, what was needed was a saint —and that is precisely who the good God had placed on the throne of St. Peter.

What were the accomplishments of this Holy Father who took as his motto: *"To restore all things in Christ"*? Perhaps one of the best ways to survey Pius X's pontificate is to do so by means of some of his encyclicals which are still so important and meaningful in our own day:

—Decree on the Necessary Dispositions for Frequent and Daily Reception of Holy Communion *(Sacra tridentina synodus)*, December 20, 1905

—On the Teaching of Christian Doctrine *(Acerbo nimis)*, April 15, 1905

—On the Age of Children Who Are To Be Admitted to First Holy Communion *(Quam singulari)*, August 8, 1910

—On the Doctrine of the Modernists *(Pascendi Dominici gregis)*, September 8, 1907, and Syllabus Condemning the Errors of the Modernists *(Lamentabili sane)*, July 3, 1907.

Pius X took over the leadership of the Catholic Church at the sunrise of the twentieth century. Along with the sun there "rose" towering problems that this Pontiff met "head-on." The Holy Father was concerned with the very deposit of the Catholic Faith, and he strove to preserve, defend and spread the message of salvation entrusted to him as supreme teacher, ruler and guide of the Church. In so doing, he has become one of the best-loved Popes of all time.

The sun began to set for Pope Pius X in the summer of 1914; the First World War was soon to be a reality. He foresaw the calamity about to prevail and strove with all his power to prevent it. Yet this, for reasons known to God, was not to be. The Pope died on August 14 of that year.

It was not until the reign of Pope John XXIII, himself a former Patriarch of Venice, that Pius X would fulfill his prophecy: "Alive or dead I will return to Venice." But fulfill it he did, because his body was for a short time returned to the people of Venice. At present the body of Pius X rests in the Chapel of the Presentation in St. Peter's Basilica. He was canonized by Pope Pius XII on May 29, 1954.

An all-encompassing description of St. Pius X, given by the head of the Catholic Institute of Paris, Monsignor Daudrillart, shortly after the Pontiff's death, is perhaps the best way to end this brief profile:

"His look, his word, his whole being expressed three things: goodness, firmness, faith. Goodness was the man himself; firmness was the leader; faith was the Christian, the priest, the Pontiff, the man of God.

"No Pope was ever more a reformer, none more modern than this fearless adversary of Modernist errors. Faithful to his watchword, he undertook to restore and renew everything in Jesus Christ.

"He was loved, tenderly loved, by the people, by all the good and simple faithful, because he was a saint, because he was a father."

Goodness Was His "Trademark"

Pope Benedict XV
(1914-1922)

For the Church and for all the world, the death of Pope Pius X was a great sorrow. Some were already saying that he was a saint, and in 1914, with the world on the brink of war, people looked anxiously to the Chair of Peter for courage and stability.

Cardinals coming from all over the world to elect a new Supreme Pontiff certainly had much to think about.

"We need a man who can help our poor world."

"Yes, and who will be a father to all people no matter what side of the war they are on."

"We need a Pope who will help negotiate peace between nations."

The Cardinals found the new Holy Father in calm, kindly Giacomo Della Chiesa. Presented with the traditional question: "Do you accept your election?" Della Chiesa thought of the immense responsibility that would be his. Putting his trust in God, he simply responded: "I accept." The new Pontiff expressed the wish to be called Benedict XV.

As a boy, Giacomo had asked his father if he could become a priest. Feeling that he had the right to arrange his son's career—as well as his marriage—Giuseppe Della Chiesa emphatically answered: "No! You will be a lawyer!"

Since his father was not one to change his mind quickly, Giacomo kept silent about his own preferences, and applied himself to the study of law. Still, Giacomo did not give up his desire for the priesthood. After receiving his doctorate in law, he again spoke to his father about his greatest hope. The elder Della Chiesa reluctantly agreed; Giacomo would go to Rome, not as a son of the noble family of Chiesa, but as an ordinary seminarian.

Ordained a priest on December 21, 1878, Father Giacomo Della Chiesa celebrated his first Mass in St. Peter's Basilica. The young priest continued his studies in theology and canon law, impressing his superiors with his ability. It was not long before he was in the papal diplomatic service. There he was made Undersecretary of State by Cardinal Rampolla, Secretary of State to Pope Leo XIII. Della Chiesa retained this position under the next Pope, Pius X, until he was appointed Archbishop of Bologna. Seven years later, in 1914, he was made a Cardinal.

Then it came: the war, the death of Pius X, the conclave which elected him Pope—everything happened so quickly. The new Pope, Benedict, set himself to work for peace, and he turned the Vatican into a center of charity for all people.

Because of the war, many families had lost contact with their dear ones. Often a mother in desperation would write to the Pope asking where her son was: "Your Holiness, I cannot find my boy. Do you know where he is? Please help me find my son!" At first, Pope Benedict answered these letters personally. When the sheer amount of similar mail made this impossible, the

Pope did the next best thing. He saw to it that a special Bureau for Prisoners of War was set up in the Vatican, of which the Pope himself was the head.

Pope Benedict took a personal interest in the individual families torn by the war which made him extremely popular with the people. His diplomatic efforts won him the esteem of all those genuinely concerned with the quest for peace. Above all, however, Benedict was a man of prayer. He knew that apart from the help of God, talks, treaties, and truces would not lead to peace. And at that very time, in Fatima, Portugal, the Blessed Virgin told three shepherd children the same thing.

The Holy Father wanted to help everyone in any way he could. When needy persons visited him, the Pope would slip his hand into his desk to give something "to help out." When he had completely exhausted his funds, his Secretary of State, Cardinal Gasparri, would ask visitors not to mention their difficulties, since His Holiness would feel deep regret at not being able to assist them. In fact, the Holy Father gave beyond his means; after his death, the Vatican had to borrow money to pay the funeral expenses.

Pope Benedict was a forerunner in his aims at unity with the Eastern Orthodox Churches.

He made it clear that Catholics of the Eastern rites are in no way inferior to those of the Latin rite. To promote the understanding of the Eastern culture and its deep religious heritage, the

Pope began an Institute for Oriental Studies. This institute was to be open to Catholic clerics of Eastern rite, clerics of the Orthodox Churches, and to Latin rite priests who wished to care for souls in the Eastern countries. Courses offered by this special Pontifical Institute included Patrology, the Eastern liturgies, and even the sacred and secular history of Byzantium and the rest of the Near and Middle East. His Holiness explained that the Church is not only Latin, Greek, or Slavonic, but *Catholic,* which means *universal.*

In 1917, on the vigil of the feast of Saints Peter and Paul, Benedict promulgated the new Code of Canon Law, the revision of which had been started by his saintly Predecessor, Pius X. This work had been an immense undertaking. Through her many years, the Church, as is her right and duty, passed laws according to various needs and situations. At a certain point, it became necessary to recodify all of this legislation. Many had tried to organize the content of canon law, but their attempts had failed. Soon after his election, Pius X began working to put all of these laws into logical order. At his death, the work fell into the hands of Pope Benedict, who also labored for three years to finish the revised Code of Canon Law. In presenting the completed work, however, Benedict characteristically gave all the credit to the man who had preceded him in the papacy.

Benedict loved the Bible and did much to encourage people to read it often. Before his elevation to the Chair of Peter, he had belonged to a society which tried to place a copy of the Sacred Book in every home. Benedict himself was very familiar with the Scriptures, and included many insights from them in his homilies, addresses and documents. His longest encyclical, *Spiritus Paraclitus,* dealt with the study and interpretation of Sacred Scripture.

In connection with his desire to make the Bible more widely known, Benedict wrote thus to Father James Alberione, founder of the Society of St. Paul and the Daughters of St. Paul: "The press is an apostolate, but for some it is business, and for others, dilettantism. It should be remembered, instead, that it is a mission."

Like all mankind, the Vicar of Christ, too, must strive to "be perfect as the heavenly Father is perfect" (Mt. 5:48). In his quest for sanctity, Benedict also found himself working to control his quick temper. But every now and then it would surface. Needless to say, the one who might have provoked the prelate was saddened and embarrassed, but the humiliation that the person felt was nothing compared to Benedict's sorrow. He never let such things go, but would immediately apologize, and would go out of his way to do some kind deed for that person.

Pope Benedict spent himself completely in the fulfillment of his duties as universal pastor. Finally, he reached the point at which there was only one thing left to give.

January 22, 1922, dawned crisp with the winter air. All of Rome—all the world—was disheartened by the morning headlines. His Holiness, Pope Benedict XV, was dead. True, he had been ill for the past few weeks, but it is never easy to accept the death of one's father. The world would miss this man of God, this man of "goodness," who had won their hearts.

Echo of the Divine Voice

Pope Pius XI

(1922-1939)

Perhaps few would ever have imagined that the son of a factory manager from Desio, Italy, would have become a future Pontiff. But that is precisely what happened in the person of Achille Ratti, known to history as Pope Pius XI. He was born on May 31, 1857. His love for learning led him toward a brilliant scholastic career from his younger years right through his seminary training at Lombard College in Rome. It was there that he was ordained a priest on December 20, 1879.

All would not be study for the young priest, however. As a student he had developed a taste and aptitude for mountain climbing. In fact, in 1889, Father Ratti and three companions scaled the heights of the 15,400-foot peak Monte Rosa on the Italo-Swiss border—the first Italians to do so.

Father Ratti soon was teaching at the seminary. He became known for his energy and dedication, two qualities that would be characteristic of him for the rest of his life. In 1889, he joined the staff of the famous Ambrosian Library. He also served as chaplain to an order of nuns in Milan, regularly taught catechism to the poor children of the city's slum areas and served the German-speaking population in a pastoral capacity.

In 1914, Pope Pius X, convinced of Ratti's goodness and gifts, put him in charge of the Vatican Library. But in 1918, his library career ended, and although it came as a surprise, Achille

Ratti accepted his appointment by Benedict XV to be apostolic envoy (and later Papal Nuncio) to Poland. The Church was in a precarious position, and the representative of the Vatican could do much for the People of God there. Even in the face of invasion, Father Ratti was not to flee Warsaw as would ambassadors of other nations. Instead, he would remain, courageous, steadfast and loyal to the Polish people—he who represented the most defenseless yet forceful "power" on earth.

Before he was recalled from Poland, Achille Ratti received episcopal ordination, much to the delight of the Polish people who loved him.

Back in Rome, in 1921, Archbishop Ratti was made a Cardinal and given charge of the Archdiocese of Milan. Despite his reputation as a scholar and intellectual, he soon proved himself to be a man of the people. But Cardinal Ratti was not to remain long in Milan. Five months later he had a new name and a new home. He had been elected Pope and had taken the name of Pius.

At this point, the outstanding qualities of Pope Pius XI noticeably surfaced. Once he was to make up his mind on a matter of primary importance—and that after careful deliberation and prayer—he would be immovable. Yet, regarding affairs of not so essential significance, he would remain a diplomat. In this light, the magnitude of his pontificate can be viewed: he was the Head of the Church as well as the sovereign head of state. He could and did condemn infringement on the rights of God and man as he vigorously denounced the elements that led and still can lead to such tragic episodes in human history.

Pius XI made more concordats (Church-State pacts) than any other Pontiff—twenty-five in his seventeen-year reign. Yes, he could negotiate, but when it came to the defense of truth, he was unflinching. Nothing meant more to the Pope than God's glory and the establishment of His sovereignty on earth. With this in mind, he inaugurated the feast of Christ the King with all its supernatural and theological implications.

One of the most outstanding examples of Pius XI's diplomatic capabilities was the Lateran Treaty of 1929 between the Vatican and Italy from which emerged the sovereign and independent Vatican City State.

Because of his zealous promotion of mission activity, Pius XI is called the Pope of the missions. Due to his efforts, mission activity continued to develop successfully especially in Asia and Africa, and there was visible growth in numbers among the native clergy. Pius XI can also be called the Pope of "Catholic Action," which he organized among the lay people.

The pontificate of Pope Pius XI lasted from 1922 to 1939. During that time, the world went through years of prosperity and economic collapse, only to emerge on the brink of war. Pius XI, whose goal was: "The peace of Christ in the kingdom of Christ," realized that if Christ's reign was to extend over the earth, He must first reign in the hearts of men. Therefore, the Pope strove with all his being to re-Christianize society and to permeate it with the love and teaching of Christ. This theme can be found time and again throughout his more than two-hundred published documents which include encyclicals, messages and letters.

Pius XI was a friend of Marconi, inventor of the wireless radio, and the Pope asked him to build a radio station for the Vatican. This Pontiff was to be the first Pope to speak to the world over the radio.

Pope Pius XI wrote: *Non Abbiamo Bisogno* and *Mit Brennender Sorge,* powerful condemnations of Church persecution and the violation of the human rights of all people. Both encyclicals had to be clandestinely released for publication. The first of these was smuggled out of the country and published abroad through the cooperation of an American monsignor named Francis Speilman.

Pius XI also wrote twenty-seven other encyclicals which reveal him to be a teacher with far-reaching vision. Wherever the voice of the Church should have been, the Vicar of Christ could be heard. His encyclicals on Christian Marriage, Christian Education of Youth, On the Social Reconstruction—written on the fortieth anniversary of Leo XIII's *Rerum novarum*—and the encyclical on Motion Pictures are still much in demand today.

The encyclical that has been called "the best of the best" is *Divini Redemptoris: On Atheistic Communism.* In that document, the Holy Father said: "In truth, it is not because men believe in

God that He exists; rather because He exists do all men whose eyes are not deliberately closed to the truth believe in Him and pray to Him."

On one occasion, Pius XI remarked: "Our motto will always be 'Know in order to live.'" During his entire pontificate, he encouraged the development of Catholic intellectual life. This was shown in the growth of the Pontifical Biblical Institute in Rome and the Biblical School of Jerusalem; the foundation of the Pontifical Academy of Sciences to which non-Catholics can also belong, and the support given to scientific, literary and juridical congresses under Catholic auspices.

As the life of Pius XI drew to a close, the world found itself in a difficult situation. The Holy Father had spent all his energies in proclaiming the voice of the divine Teacher, and despite severe pain, as the eighty-second year of his life continued, he told his doctors: "The Pope cannot be ill. The Pope is in the hands of God who will call him in His own good time. We shall continue to work until called." After an illness of two and a half years, God beckoned him home. This man of God, who had never ceased to proclaim all that Christ *is* and *taught,* died peacefully on February 10, 1939.

Pius pp. XII

"Pacelli"—His Name Means "Peace"

Pope Pius XII
(1939-1958)

July 9, 1943. Low-flying bombers left the Tibertine section of Rome in turmoil. Less than an hour after the attack, a white-clad figure was seen bending, busily attending to the needs of his flock. Pope Pius XII, having drawn a large amount of money from the Vatican Bank, walked the streets with Monsignor Montini, the future Pope Paul VI, bringing whatever comfort and relief he could to the victims. His cassock was soon stained with blood as his frightened children pressed against him; just his presence was enough to calm them. Someone in the crowd threw a jacket on the ground. The Pope knelt on it and joined them in prayer for peace and safety.

World War II was not to end for another two years despite the continual efforts of this Pope of peace. "Nothing is lost by peace," he cautioned, "all can be lost through war."

Pope Pius XII was born on March 2, 1876, and christened Eugenio Pacelli. Sixty-three years later, to the day, he would be elected to the Chair of St. Peter. Located in Rome, the heart of Christendom, the Pacelli home was a center of deep Catholic devotion. Virginia Pacelli fostered great love for the Blessed Virgin Mary in her young son, a love which grew stronger through the years. One day he would have the joy of proclaiming the dogma of her Assumption, body and soul, into heaven.

As a youth, Eugenio wondered about his vocation in life. The practice of law had been a tradition in the family and Eugenio knew he had the capacity for it. Still, the desire to become a priest would not leave him. After a four-day retreat, eighteen-year-old Eugenio knew what he would do. He would give his all to God without reserve.

In 1894, he entered the Capranica College to begin his studies for the priesthood. Did this young seminarian have any idea of what lay ahead of him? God gives the grace for each moment of our life as it comes, and little by little He prepared Eugenio for the heavy burden he would carry as universal Father of the Church.

Besides his regular studies at the college, Eugenio took on extra courses at the Gregorian University. After graduation, Eugenio went to the Pontifical University of the Roman Seminary. Once more he outdid himself. On his graduation day, Pope Leo XIII summoned Pacelli to his office to congratulate him.

April 2, 1899, marked the most glorious Easter of the young man's life; it was his ordination day. Father Pacelli celebrated his first Mass the following day in the Church of St. Mary Major, the largest Marian shrine in the world. He entrusted his priesthood to Mary as he had entrusted his youth.

Father Pacelli's first assignment was in the parish of the Chiesa Nuova, where as a young student he had served as an altar boy. He loved his work there! Much of his time was spent

teaching catechism to the children and listening
to their first attempts at saying their prayers. The
children flocked around him and Father Pacelli
answered their every question. How often as he
gazed down at them must he have thought of the
words of Jesus: "Let the little children come to
me. Do not shut them off. The reign of God
belongs to such as these" (Lk. 18:16).

Father Pacelli would have been content to
continue at the Chiesa Nuova for the rest of his
days, but he was not long for parish work. Only
two years after ordination, he was asked to accept
a position in the Vatican foreign office by Monsignor Gasparri, Secretary of the Congregation of
Extraordinary Ecclesiastical Affairs. Monsignor
had been watching the priest and knew his poten
tial. It took some convincing but Monsignor
Gasparri finally managed to prevail.

At the Vatican Father Pacelli was given various assignments to which he applied himself
with the intensity and fervor so characteristic of
his youth.

With the start of World War I the Vatican
became a relief station for the suffering prisoners
of war. Thirty-thousand French and German
prisoners were returned to their homes due to
the efforts of the Vatican. The responsibility for
this task fell on the shoulders of the now Monsignor Pacelli, the new Secretary of the Congregation of Extraordinary Ecclesiastical Affairs.

Before the end of the war, Monsignor Pacelli
was chosen for the difficult position of Papal
Nuncio to Munich. Pope Benedict XV conse-

crated him a bishop, and he left on this delicate mission. Later he was made Papal Nuncio to Berlin. Both of these posts were a test of the Archbishop's courage and tact. Despite threats against the Church and his own person, he would not budge from doing his duty. Seeing his efforts for peace rejected by the government, he turned to doing good to those who needed him most. Tirelessly, he brought food and clothing to those left destitute by World War I. For thirteen years he labored among the German people until 1930, when he was called to Rome. For his departure, the government provided an open carriage to take him to the railroad station. As he was driven along, the Archbishop could not suppress his emotion. On each side of his carriage, thousands and thousands of people were lined up with torches in hand to light his way. They called out their love and affection as he drove by. Archbishop Pacelli stood up and blessed his flock as he passed. He and they wept.

In Rome, Archbishop Pacelli was made a Cardinal and appointed Secretary of State under Pope Pius XI. He strove to be of one mind with the Supreme Pontiff in everything and the Pope affirmed that Cardinal Pacelli truly was his "other self," and again, "Cardinal Pacelli speaks with my voice."

In February of 1939, Pope Pius XI died. It was a difficult time for the Church. World War II was fast approaching. Who would steer the Bark of Peter through the stormy waters ahead? The Holy Spirit, at work through the conclave, chose Cardinal Pacelli. Out of great love and admiration for his Predecessor, the new Pontiff took the name of Pope Pius XII. He who had so thoroughly penetrated the ideals and goals of the great Pope Pius XI would guide the Church on the same sure course with equal valor.

All during his first summer as Pope, Pius XII worked to prevent the war. His efforts bore little fruit. As soon as World War II began, the Vatican started its relief programs. Clothes, food and medicine were shipped to the needy. Families were helped to locate their missing relatives. Thousands of Jews, hunted by Hitler, found refuge in tiny Vatican City State. After the war, a number of them, impressed by the great charity of the Pope, embraced the Catholic Faith, including the chief rabbi of Rome, Eugenio Zolli.

After both bombings of Rome, Pope Pius XII went out himself to comfort his people. Four small bombs were even dropped on the Vatican itself, in an attempt to force the Pope to leave the city. He refused. He was a shepherd who would remain with his flock no matter the cost.

After the war, Pope Pius XII dedicated himself all the more intensely to Church matters. His reforms in various areas of ecclesiastical life prepared the way for Vatican Council II. Forty-one encyclical letters were issued during his pontificate. The Holy Year of 1950, the proclamation of the dogma of the Assumption on November 1, 1950, and the Marian Year of 1954 were also achievements of his reign. On August 12, 1950, he issued the powerful encyclical

Humani generis in which the Pope stated: "The truths that have to do with God and the relations between God and men completely surpass the sensible order and demand self-surrender and self-abnegation in order to be put into practice and to influence practical life...." These words touched the conscience of a weary world because Christ's Vicar lived what he taught.

His Holiness will forever be remembered with gratitude by the Daughters of St. Paul because it was Pope Pius XII who granted their Congregation final papal approval.

On mention of Pope Pius XII, many think of a man of genius, which indeed he was. From his earliest school years this gift was evident as he excelled in Greek and Latin as well as in modern languages. Many think of a man of deep spirituality. They call him saintly, angelic, mystical, which he was. But there was another side to the Pope as well—a side which caused him to treasure moments with young children in the general audiences, to take an interest in anyone who visited the Vatican and be able to converse knowledgeably with them on almost any subject, to cry all the way back to the Vatican after visiting the victims of a bombing.

The life of Pope Pius XII, a great gift to our century, ended on October 9, 1958. May all people everywhere be as dedicated to the cause of peace as was this Pope, inspired by the words of Jesus: "Blest too the peacemakers; they shall be called sons of God" (Mt. 5:9).

Everybody's Father

Pope John XXIII
(1958-1963)

Angelo Giuseppe Roncalli was born on November 25, 1881, in the mountain region of northern Italy. One of thirteen children, he grew up in a poor but cheerful atmosphere, where farming, fresh air, and play kept the children busy and happy.

Angelo was enrolled in a local school, not far from the Roncalli home. This meant a big sacrifice for his parents, but they wanted the best for their oldest son. Angelo's day would start with class, but the afternoons were devoted to work in the fields, the afternoon rosary, and of course, a game or two.

As much as he enjoyed games and jokes, young Roncalli gave prayer an important place in his life. The thought of becoming a priest, too, was one of the boy's greatest aspirations. After receiving Jesus for the first time in Holy Communion, Angelo felt even more strongly the call to the priesthood.

At the age of fourteen, Angelo entered the seminary in Bergamo. He adapted extremely well to seminary life, and seemed to mature both emotionally and spiritually. The young seminarian applied himself diligently to his studies, and was allowed to finish his training at the Pontifical Apollinare Seminary in Rome. It was here that he began writing his experiences and spiritual reflections in a diary which would later be published as *Journal of a Soul*.

Honest, straightforward and kind, Angelo's most outstanding attribute was still his sense of humor. Even though the passing years added new responsibilities, he never lost his keen wit. He managed to cultivate it into a real virtue!

Finally, in 1904, Angelo was ordained. He offered his first Mass in St. Peter's Basilica in Rome. Father Roncalli was then assigned to be secretary to Bishop Radini-Tedeschi at Bergamo. He later taught apologetics and Church history at the Seminary of Bergamo.

Not even the outbreak of World War I could stop the active young priest. Roncalli served God and country as a sergeant in the Medical Corps, and later as a lieutenant of the Chaplains' Corps. After the war, Father Angelo went back home... but not for long.

When, in 1925, Pope Pius XI found himself in need of a representative to serve the Catholic community in Bulgaria, it was the zealous and likeable Father Roncalli whom he chose. Ordained a bishop and elevated to the rank of archbishop, Roncalli spent eighteen years laboring on the Church's behalf in that country. Witnessing the wonderful impression Archbishop Roncalli made on the Bulgarian people, the Pope appointed him Apostolic Delegate to Greece, Istanbul and Turkey. Because of his wit and kindness in handling situations, Roncalli became known as an excellent diplomat.

Even though most did not share his Catholic Faith, the people of Greece and Turkey grew very fond of the Apostolic Delegate. While in those countries, Archbishop Roncalli made it clear that every moment of his time was at the disposal of the people.

Much of the Archbishop's energies were spent in fervent attempts to heal the severed ties between the Roman Catholic Church and the Eastern Orthodox. For their part, the Orthodox people sensed Roncalli's deep-rooted concern for this reunion. Under Pope Pius XII, Archbishop Roncalli also served as Papal Nuncio to France.

In 1953, Pope Pius XII gave the now seventy-two-year-old Archbishop yet another title of honor and responsibility: he was created a Cardinal and assigned the Patriarchate of Venice. Five years after Cardinal Roncalli received the red hat, Pope Pius XII died. The Catholic flock was in need of a shepherd.

Never suspecting what was to happen there, Cardinal Roncalli joined the other Cardinals in the conclave. After three days, the Cardinal-deacon appeared with the name of the next Successor of St. Peter—Angelo Cardinal Roncalli, who would be called Pope John XXIII.

The news media was continually showing this dynamic Pope "in action." People couldn't help but feel affection for this holy man of God.

Pope John did not find it easy to adapt to an age-old custom according to which the Pope was to dine alone. Approximately one week following his election to the Papacy, His Holiness decided to start his own tradition of inviting friends to dinner.

The Holy Father was also reverently referred to by many as "John outside the walls." It was not unusual for Pope John to spontaneously leave the Vatican and visit one of the local hospitals. He also visited the prisons of Rome, so that he could speak to and counsel the inmates. In both examples, one sees the corporal and spiritual works of mercy practiced by this fatherly Pontiff.

Pope John also enjoyed conversing with the Vatican's grounds crew. It is said that the Pope noticed how tired a hard-working gardener looked after a strenuous morning. Pope John decided to invite him to share an afternoon snack. Needless to say, the groundskeeper was elated with His Holiness' company.

But although Pope John enjoyed these moments with individual members of his flock, he never forgot his responsibility for the entire Church. His deep concern for the spiritual vitality of the Church and his realization of the Church's need for interior renewal led this dynamic Pope to announce the opening of the Second Vatican Council.

Pope John had great hopes for the Council. He wanted Vatican II to help all people recognize the Catholic Church as the presence of Christ in modern society. He desired that the Council strengthen Catholics whose faith had been shaken by the reappearance of Modernism. The Holy Father hoped, too, that this Council would bring to our separated brethren a deeper understanding of the Church's beliefs and a fuller appreciation of those things which they already hold in common with the Catholic Church.

On October 11, 1962, the Second Vatican Ecumenical Council began. Pope John did not live to see its completion. After reigning five and a half years, the Pontiff announced: "My bags are packed" and surrendered his soul to the crucified Master. The Pope's death was extremely painful, but he offered his sufferings for the success of the Council. That offering must have been accepted because it was easy to see the Providence of God and the action of the Holy Spirit at work in the choice of Pope John's Successor—Giovanni Battista Montini—Pope Paul VI.

Pope John XXIII's brief reign made a lasting impact on the Church and on the world. His love for all people, whether or not they shared his Faith, evoked from all a response of love. Pope John saw the good in everyone because he looked at all with the gentle eyes of Christ.

Pope John Paul II Calls Him... Paul "The Great"

Pope Paul VI
(1963-1978)

"Convinced of Jesus Christ:
I feel the need to proclaim Him;
I cannot keep silent. 'Woe to me
if I do not preach the Gospel!' (1 Cor. 9:16)

I am sent by Him, by Christ Himself,
to do this.
I am an apostle; I am a witness.
The more distant the goal,
the more difficult my mission,
the more pressing is the love
that urges me to it (cf. 2 Cor. 5:14).
I must bear witness to His name."

These are the words of Pope Paul VI which reveal the interior force that sustained him through many and prolonged trials. What was this force? It was a deep, irrevocable and overflowing love for Jesus Christ and His Body, the Church.

Giovanni Battista Montini, born September 26, 1897, in Concesio, Italy, was the second son of George and Judith Montini. At the age of eighteen, Giovanni confided to his friend, Father Persico, that he wished to become a priest. He entered the seminary, studied hard and spent his free time teaching catechism to the children preparing for First Holy Communion and Confirmation.

On May 29, 1920, Giovanni was ordained a priest. The next day he celebrated his first Mass in

Brescia where his father and mother experienced the joy of receiving Communion from the hands of their son. Father Montini was assigned as curate in the village of Verdanuova. His days there, however, were to be few. In the autumn of that year, he was sent to Rome for further studies at the Academy of Ecclesiastical Nobles.

As time went on, Father Montini was assigned various responsibilities in the Vatican. Even though he loved the work he was doing, Father Giovanni longed to be with the people—the laborers, the poor, the handicapped, the suffering. He expressed this desire to Monsignor Pizzardo, who then appointed him spiritual director of the Roman branch of FUCI (Italian Federation of Catholic University Students), a post which he held from 1924-1934. Montini loved this assignment. The students affectionately called him "Don (Father) G.B.M." He would give them his time and they would freely ask him questions about religion, morality, philosophy, theology. "Don G.B.M." organized and strengthened FUCI. Its members, under Father Montini's guidance, continued to work to keep Italian students at a high moral level.

During the Second World War, the man who was to become a future Pontiff worked closely with Pope Pius XII to help the Jews and other war refugees. At this time, Montini established and managed the largest relief program for refugees ever to have existed in the history of the Church. After the war, Pope Pius XII depended on Monsignor Montini as his chief diplomat. In

1954, Giovanni Battista Montini became Archbishop of Milan and was to spend eight years there.

When John XXIII became Pope, he elevated Archbishop Montini to the rank of Cardinal and relied heavily on him in the preparations for Vatican Council II. Scarcely had the Council gotten under way when Pope John was called home to God. On June 16, 1963, Cardinal Montini went with the other Cardinals into the conclave. He emerged two days later as Pope John's Successor.

Cardinal Montini chose to be named after the great Apostle to the nations, St. Paul. Even though nearly two thousand years would separate them in time, they would have so much in common, these two men called *Paul*.

Besides the ordinary burdens of the Papacy, the new Pope had "inherited" an ecumenical council. He took his responsibilities to heart. Pope Paul VI personally guided the Council's completion and implementation. He promulgated its sixteen documents. This Pope, like his Predecessors, made great steps in diplomacy and in ecumenism. He became a traveling Pope and worked tirelessly for peace.

During his fifteen years as Pope, Paul VI visited every continent except Antarctica. He attended a Eucharistic Congress in Bombay, India, in 1964; delivered a powerful address at the U.N. on October 4, 1965; visited the shrine of Our Lady of Fatima in Portugal, as well as another Marian shrine at Ephesus in Turkey, in 1967; and attended another Eucharistic Congress in Bogota, Colombia, in 1968. In 1969, he flew to Geneva, Switzerland, to address the International Labor Organization and the leaders of the World Council of Churches. Later that year, he made a pilgrimage to Uganda in Africa, to pray at the shrines of the Uganda martyrs.

The last of Pope Paul's trips outside Italy was undertaken in 1970, when he was seventy-three years old. During ten intense days he traveled to Tehran, Iran; Dacca, East Pakistan; Manila in the Philippines; Samoa; Sydney, Australia; Djakarta, Indonesia; Hong Kong; and Colombo, Ceylon.

Everywhere the presence of Pope Paul renewed faith, instilled hope and trust and reawakened brotherly love in the hearts of men.

The Pontiff's greatest achievement—true to his namesake, Paul—is revealed in his steadfast defense of the deposit of Divine Revelation which is still under attack even in our day.

From his monumental writings, which have led men of vision to call him: "Paul the Great," we can see how he defended Church doctrine and in so doing, defended the rights of all people: Paths of the Church *(Ecclesiam suam)* on fidelity to the Christian life; Mystery of Faith *(Mysterium Fidei)* on the Holy Eucharist; The Credo of the People of God (the basic truths of the Catholic Faith proclaimed); Of Human Life *(Humanae vitae)* on the sacredness of human life; On Evangelization in the Modern World *(Evangelii nuntiandi)* on our obligation to communicate the Gospel message to all; Priestly Celibacy *(Sacerdotalis caelibatus);* For the Right Ordering and

Development of Devotion to the Blessed Virgin Mary *(Marialis cultus);* On the Development of Peoples *(Populorum progressio)* on the Church's concern for developing nations; On Christian Joy *(Gaudete in Domino)* on the Christian's ability to find tranquillity even amidst sufferings; On the Renewal of Religious Life According to the Teaching of the Second Vatican Council *(Evangelica testificatio),* etc.

In the turbulent aftermath of post-conciliar years, Pope Paul VI had a grave challenge to meet. It involved a choice: to stand firm with Christ and defend Church teachings, or to give in to pressures for compromise from individuals and groups both within and outside the Church. Giving a marvelous witness of fidelity to Truth, Pope Paul placed conscience before popularity, and the law of God before the approval of men. Because of this, like St. Paul, he suffered greatly.

During one of his regular Wednesday afternoon general audiences, Pope Paul VI asked the crowd:

> "Will we forget that the Church, also in her suffering, and precisely because of such suffering, experiences at once the consolations of God and 'overflows with joy in all' [her] 'troubles'? (2 Cor. 7:4)

> "Will we not perhaps love our Mother, holy Church, the more precisely because she is suffering?

> "This is the invitation we extend to all of you, together with our apostolic blessing."

Scholar, diplomat and man of spiritual depth, Paul VI was also a person of warmth and understanding. He quietly manifested a most delicate sense of human feeling. During his trip to India in 1964, Pope Paul visited an orphanage. The children were very impressed. At Mass, the Holy Father had personally distributed Communion to each child, and now he was in their dining room, eating with them.

One of the little boys, Tony Mascarenas, expressed the feelings of all: "We have no daddy and no mommy; we have nobody. But the Church is our Mother and you are our Father."

The Pope replied with great tenderness: "I have come from Rome to see you and to tell you how much I love you, just like your father." With these words, he united all of us in the embrace of his paternal love. He seemed to be telling all of God's children: "I love you, just like your father."

In this brief chapter on the person and Papacy of Giovanni Battista Montini, we ask ourselves: What, then, is the legacy of Pope Paul VI? He has shared with us his genius, his energies, his important encyclicals and documents, his virtues, his balance, his courage, his patience and his tremendous love. The late Cardinal Wright said that he "had the mind of Peter and the heart of Paul." But the most valuable part of the legacy is his commitment to the total content of divine Revelation, pure and unabridged, available to anyone "who believes that Jesus is the Son of God" (1 Jn. 5:4-5). Kind but firm, Pope Paul guarded that legacy from innovators, from the hireling shepherds, who do not have the interests of Christ's Church as their own.

So it was that on June 19, 1978, the fifteenth anniversary of his pontificate, Paul VI was able to say with the Apostle Paul, " 'I have kept the faith! I have kept the faith!' we can say today, with the humble but firm consciousness of never having betrayed the holy truth."

The legacy of Paul VI, then, is the Catholic Faith, our heritage.

His Holiness
POPE JOHN PAUL I
August 26, 1978
September 28, 1978

"If all the sons and daughters of the Church would know how to be tireless missionaries of the Gospel, a new flowering holiness and renewal would spring up in this world that thirsts for love and for truth."
— POPE JOHN PAUL I

". . . his soul being pleasing to the Lord, He has taken him quickly . . ." (Wisdom 4:14)

 THE SOCIETY FOR THE PROPAGATION OF THE FAITH

Diocese of Fresno
1550 North Fresno
Fresno, California 93703
Rev. Msgr. Denis J. Doherty
Director

Pope of the Smile

Pope John Paul I

(1978—Supreme Pontiff
for thirty-four days)

From the balcony, the Cardinal-deacon smiled on the excited, anticipating crowd. After one of the briefest conclaves in history, the flock of Christ heard again the consoling message: "I announce a great joy! We have a Pope, the most eminent...Cardinal Luciani, who has chosen the name of *John Paul*." The crowd thundered their applause. The humble and fatherly Patriarch of Venice, chosen by God for the See of St. Peter, later admitted that he had neither the "wisdom of the heart" of Pope John, or the preparation and culture of Pope Paul VI, but that he hoped that through the prayers of the people, he would be able to serve the Church. It was soon clear that the new Pope would have both the prayers and affection of all people of good will.

Albino Luciani was born on October 12, 1912, in a brick mountain farmhouse. His socialist father did not object to the boy's baptism which took place a few days after birth. It was from their devout mother that Albino and his brothers and sisters learned the Catholic Faith.

At twelve years of age, Albino entered the nearby seminary to begin the first studies toward his goal of priestly ordination. His years of preparation were completed at the major seminary of Belluno. Ordination day came on July 7, 1935. His bishop designated Luciani for further studies in philosophy and theology at the Gregorian

University in Rome. He received his doctorate in theology within two years, and then returned to serve the people of his hometown parish. For ten years, the young priest filled the roles of parish priest, high school teacher, seminary professor. Father Luciani's many abilities: his candor, his wholesome affability, quick wit and intelligence did not long remain hidden. He was ordained a bishop by Pope John XXIII in 1958. For his coat of arms, Bishop Luciani's motto was: "Humility."

Eleven years later, Paul VI chose Luciani to head the prestigious See of Venice. His gentleness and interest in the people won their affection. A great administrator, Archbishop Luciani erected new parishes to provide spiritual support. By working with the civil authorities, Luciani was able to ensure that the needs of the poor and jobless would be met.

It was in Venice that Archbishop Luciani wrote the now famous *Illustrissimi*, a series of imaginary letters to great, "illustrious" people in history and literature. The humor and insight in these written reflections made them a very appealing way for adults to renew their knowledge of the Faith.

In September, 1972, the Archbishop of Venice and his flock were blessed with a visit by Pope Paul VI. It was then, in St. Mark's Square, before twenty thousand of the Venetian faithful, that the most embarrassing moment in Luciani's life occurred. Pope Paul VI, smiling, removed his stole, ancient symbol of authority, and carefully placed it over the shoulders of the Patriarch of Venice. The jubilant crowd interpreted this as a sign that their beloved archbishop would soon receive the red hat of a Cardinal. But in view of the events that would take place in 1978—the year of the three Popes—the gesture had even more significance.

In March, 1973, Paul VI elevated Albino Luciani to the dignity of a Cardinal. Always at home with the poor, the Archbishop of Venice loved to visit his flock. The Venetian people frequently saw their Patriarch on his bicycle, going to visit the families in his diocese.

Then came the warm, August day of 1978. The Cardinals of the Roman Catholic Church assembled to elect a Successor to the heroic Paul VI. The Holy Spirit made His choice known rather early in the conclave: Albino Luciani.

And so it was. The burden of authority passed from the shoulders of Pope Paul VI to John Paul I, and with the authority came the abundance of God's grace. Luciani became the first Pope in history to bear a double name. But how could he have chosen between the two Popes, John XXIII and Paul VI? The day following his election to the Supreme Pontificate, His Holiness explained:

"Pope John had decided to consecrate me himself in St. Peter's Basilica; then, however unworthy, I succeeded him in Venice on the Chair of St. Mark, in that Venice which is still full of Pope John....

"Then, Pope Paul made me a Cardinal. Furthermore, during his fifteen years of pontificate, this Pope has shown, not only to me but to the whole world, how to love, how to serve, how to labor and how to suffer for the Church of Christ. For that reason I said: 'I shall be called John Paul.' "

As did his Predecessor, John Paul I used his Wednesday general audiences to instruct the faithful. His fatherly talks centered around the virtues: humility, faith, hope, charity. In his concern for the spread of the Gospel, Papa Luciani exhorted the faithful: "If all the sons and daughters of the Church would know how to be tireless missionaries of the Gospel, a new flowering of holiness and renewal would spring up in this world."

The reign of Pope John Paul I offered the Church the bright promise of peace and progress. No one dreamed that Papa Luciani (who at age sixty-five was considered young) would be the "September Pope," or that his reign might be called the "September Papacy." Yet, it would be.

On Friday, September 29, 1978, Father John McGee, the Pope's secretary, prayed silently in the papal chapel. It was 5:30 a.m. The priestly vestments were prepared on the altar; Pope John Paul usually began each day at this hour by offering the Holy Mass. Nervously wondering why the Holy Father was not on schedule, the priest walked quickly to the Pontiff's room and knocked on the door. No response. Father McGee slowly entered the room and saw that the Pope was in bed. The reading light was still on, and a book, the *Imitation of Christ*, was in his hands. But the Pope was not reading; in the quiet of the night he had surrendered his soul to the heavenly Father.

The sad news of the Pope's death stunned the entire world. Catholics and non-Catholics alike would sorely miss the fatherly man whose serene smile had told them how much they were loved. Although the reign of Pope John Paul I was so brief, he prepared the way for the dynamic Pontificate of Pope John Paul II. In August, 1978, after the death of Pope Paul, as the Cardinals had filed into the conclave, one in particular had been singled out for an interview by an American newsman. Karol Cardinal Wojtyla had been asked what his "chances" were for election. The Cardinal had chuckled and quipped: "The world is not ready for a Polish Pope!" Perhaps at that moment it was not, but in the designs of Providence, a month later it would be. The reign of Pope John Paul I had paved the way.

God's Gift to Us

Pope John Paul II
Gloriously Reigning...

Born May 18, 1920, Karol Jozef Wojtyla was the younger son of a mother who predicted a glorious future for her boy but would not live to see it. Emilia Wojtyla died at the age of forty-five; Karol was nine years old at the time. Three years later, Karol accepted the death of his older brother Edmund with a faith unusually strong for a boy of twelve.

Edmund's death left Karol and his father as one another's mutual support. The years they spent together allowed the elder Wojtyla's fine example of prayer and trust to make a strong impression on Karol.

In 1938, father and son moved to the large city of Krakow, where Karol continued his education. Shortly after Karol received his degree, Poland was paralyzed by the German takeover. Karol found employment at the Solvay Chemical Works. In his spare time, he met with friends interested in preserving the Polish literary and dramatic heritage. Because this was not approved of by the Nazis, the group had to meet secretly in private homes.

It was about this time, too, that Karol became acquainted with Jan Tyranowski, a remarkable man, by profession a tailor. It may come as a surprise to most to find out that Karol learned the elements of spirituality from a layman. In fact, Tyranowski was the moderator of a group of fifteen young men who gathered to say the rosary.

In itself, this was potentially dangerous. The Germans would have found it hard to believe that those strong, young, patriotic Poles were meeting only to say prayers. But pray they did.

Tyranowski guided the youths in a program directed at developing a solid spiritual life. They followed a schedule of prayer, labor and spiritual work with the aim of growing in similarity to Christ.

In 1942, some time after his father's death, Karol was accepted as a seminarian by Archbishop Sapieha of Krakow. Externally, however, the young man's life did not change much (the German forces had forbidden entrance into the seminary). So Karol continued to live as a young worker, finding, in the slower pace of Solvay's night shift, time to study theology and philosophy.

Within two years, danger was on the increase. Without warning soldiers would march through the streets, arresting men and boys at random. Karol and the others who shared his high aspirations were brought to the Archbishop's residence. Despite the difficult circumstances, they managed to follow the seminary schedule of Mass, meditation and classes.

Karol excelled in all of his classes. The teachers were impressed and communicated their admiration to the Archbishop. Sapieha nodded with satisfaction. The reports given by Karol's professors matched his own opinion of the young man's qualities.

Wojtyla's ordination date was advanced so that as a priest Karol could go to Rome for further training in theology and philosophy. And so on November 1, 1946, in the Archbishop's chapel, Karol Wojtyla was ordained to the priesthood.

After completing doctoral studies at the Angelicum (a pontifical university staffed by the Dominicans), Father Wojtyla was appointed curate in a small parish somewhat remote from Krakow. Here the future Pontiff acquired his first pastoral experiences. He was also able to arrange retreats for young people by way of informal hiking trips since the government allowed only communist youth groups to be formed.

By 1953, Father Wojtyla was back in Krakow, this time teaching both in the seminary and at the Catholic University. He still found time to guide retreats for teenagers and also to write poetry (some of which was published under a pseudonym).

At the age of thirty-eight, Karol was named auxiliary bishop of Krakow. The youngest bishop in Poland managed to fulfill well his duties in the diocese, which included what we today call "youth ministry," at the same time continuing to teach on the university level.

All the while, he was deepening in himself both knowledge and a profound spirit of prayer. Everyone knew that prayer had first place with Bishop Wojtyla. To this most important duty he dedicated several hours each day, as well as any spare minutes he might have. Those who happened to see Wojtyla walking from one room to the next were very likely to see a rosary in his hand. Traveling time, too, was used for prayer and work. Bishop Wojtyla learned to put every available moment to good use.

The opening of Vatican Council II found Bishop Karol in Rome. He attended every session of the Council. The comments and interventions Wojtyla gave before the assembly were remarkable for their pastoral sensitiveness and depth of thought. Many of the participants began to look with great respect upon the young Polish bishop.

In December, 1963, Paul VI appointed Karol Wojtyla Archbishop of Krakow. With that honor fell the heavy responsibility of upholding, defending and promoting the Catholic Faith and the rights of Catholics in the face of a regime which persistently worked to undermine his efforts. In this, however, the young Archbishop had a strong ally: Stefan Cardinal Wyszynski, Archbishop of Warsaw, a living symbol of the Church's role of upholding the dignity and freedom of every human being.

After four years, on June 28, 1967, Karol Wojtyla was raised by Pope Paul VI to the dignity of a Cardinal. He heard the holy Pontiff recite the formula reminding the new Cardinal that he must be ready even to shed his blood for the Faith. (Little did anyone realize that in Wojtyla's case, the traditional reminder would be almost prophetic.)

The Cardinal Archbishop of Krakow continued to serve the Church with dedication and enthusiasm. In 1971, he and several other Cardinals were privileged to concelebrate with Pope Paul VI the Mass of beatification of Maximilian Kolbe, a Polish Franciscan martyred by the Nazis. Eleven years after his beatification, Pope John Paul II would himself have the joy of canonizing his fellow countryman.

Wojtyla also visited the United States twice as a Cardinal. His first visit (in 1969) was especially directed to Polish groups in America. In 1976, he returned for the International Eucharistic Congress in Philadelphia. The theme of the Congress was "The Eucharist and the Hungers of the Human Family." Wojtyla's talk regarding man's hunger for freedom was delivered in fluent English, with the Slavic accent which would soon become so familiar to his listeners.

After each of his journeys, he returned to his beloved Krakow. Karol Wojtyla was a real son of Poland. He loved her people, her villages, her mountains, and above all, her Queen, the Madonna of Czestochowa. Only for her and for her divine Son did he ever make the sacrifice of leaving his native land.

In August, 1978, at the death of Paul VI, Cardinal Wojtyla was called to Rome to elect a new Pope. After offering his promise of loyalty and the support of his prayers to the new Pontiff, John Paul I, Karol returned to his homeland, but not for long. Pope Luciani's sudden death left the chair of Peter vacant. Cardinal Wojtyla made arrangements for another trip to Rome. This time, the Madonna would ask a bigger sacrifice. Only for her would Karol say "yes."

"Habemus Papam!" "We have a Pope!" The impact of this Papal election would be felt around the world.

Papal Pronouncements*

POPE LEO XII

Condition of the Working Classes (Rerum novarum) 25¢ — EP0240

On Jesus Christ Our Redeemer (Tametsi Futura Prospicientibus) 40¢ — EP0679

On the Restoration of Christian Philosophy (Aeterni Patris) 25¢ — EP0865

On the Study of Sacred Scripture (Providentissimus Deus) 25¢ — EP0870

Unity of the Church 25¢ — EP1090

POPE PIUS X

On the Doctrine of the Modernists and Syllabus Condemning the Errors of the Modernists (Pascendi Dominici Gregis and Lamentabili sane) 50¢ — EP0860

On the Teaching of Christian Doctrine (Acerbo Nimis) 20¢ — EP0145

POPE BENEDICT XV

On the Fifteenth Centenary of the Death of St. Jerome (Spiritus Paraclitus) 35¢ — EP0487

POPE PIUS XI

Atheistic Communism (Divini Redemptoris) 25¢ — EP0160
Christian Education of Youth 25¢ — EP0189
Christian Marriage (Casti connubii) 25¢ — EP0190
Motion Pictures (Vigilanti cura) 15¢ — EP0770
Social Reconstruction (Quadragesimo anno) 25¢ — EP1020

---

*For a complete listing, write to one of the addresses at the end of this book.

POPE PIUS XII

Addresses to Cloistered Religious $1.25 — EP0020

The Assumption of the Blessed Virgin Mary (Munificentissimus Deus) 15¢ — EP0150

Dogma of the Immaculate Conception 15¢ — EP0440

Function of the State in the Modern World 25¢ — EP0500

Holy Virginity 15¢ — EP0560

Humani Generis 15¢ — EP0580

The Mystical Body of Christ (Mystici corporis Christi) 50¢ — EP0810

On Motion Pictures, Radio and Television (Miranda prorsus) 25¢ — EP0890

Promotion of Biblical Studies (Divino afflante Spiritu) 25¢ — EP0970

The Sacred Liturgy (Mediator Dei) 50¢ — EP0980

Sponsa Christi $1.00 — EP1025

POPE JOHN XXIII

Christmas Message 5¢ — EP0210

From the Beginning of Our Priesthood (Sacerdotii nostri primordia) 25¢ — EP0490

Grateful Memory (Grata recordatio) 15¢ — EP0520

Christianity and Social Progress (Mater et magistra) 50¢ — EP0200

Near the Chair of Peter (Ad Petri cathedram) 25¢ — EP0820

A Call for the Practice of Penance (Paenitentiam agere) 15¢ — EP0180

Peace Message 5¢ — EP0945

Peace on Earth (Pacem in terris) 25¢ — EP0950

To Women Religious 15¢ — EP1070

POPE PAUL VI

Address on Seminaries and Vocations (Summi Dei Verbum) 20¢ — EP0010

Apostolic Exhortation to All Bishops in Peace and Communion with the Apostolic See, on the Fifth Anniversary of the Close of the Second Vatican Council 20¢ — EP0100

Apostolic Exhortation for the Right Ordering and Development of Devotion to the Blessed Virgin Mary (Marialis cultus) 35¢ — EP0080

Apostolic Letter to Cardinal Maurice Roy, President of the Council of the Laity and of the Pontifical Commission on Justice and Peace, on the Occasion of the Eightieth

Anniversary of the Encyclical Rerum novarum ("The Coming Eightieth") (Octogesima adveniens) 25¢ — EP0230

Credo of the People of God 10¢ — EP0270

The Development of Peoples (Populorum progressio) 25¢ — EP0410

Great Sign (Signum magnum) 15¢ — EP0530

Heights of Heroism in the Life of Pius XII 5¢ — EP0550

Message to Priests 10¢ — EP0740

Month of May (Mense Maio) 15¢ — EP0760

Mystery of Faith (Mysterium fidei) 25¢ — EP0800

New Horizons for Women Religious 15¢ — EP0830

Of Human Life (Humanae vitae) 15¢ — EP0840

On Christian Joy (Gaudete in Domino) 30¢ — EP0880

On Evangelization in the Modern World (Evangelii Nuntiandi) 40¢ — EP0850

Paths of the Church (Ecclesiam Suam) 25¢ — EP0940

Priestly Celibacy (Sacerdotalis caelibatus) 25¢ — EP0960

Priests Should Be in the World, Not of the World 10¢ — EP0959

To All Religious 15¢ — EP1060

POPE JOHN PAUL II

Address of Pope John Paul II to the General Assembly of the United Nations 30¢ — EP0005

Apostolic Constitution on Ecclesiastical Universities and Faculties (Sapientia Christiana) 50¢ — EP0847

Apostolic Exhortation on Catechesis in Our Time (Catechesi tradendae) 60¢ — EP0185

For the 1600th Anniversary of the First Council of Constantinople and the 1550th Anniversary of the Council of Ephesus 30¢ — EP0486

The Freedom of Conscience and Religion 25¢ — EP0489

Instruction Concerning Worship of the Eucharistic Mystery 25¢ — EP0605

Letter to All Bishops of the Church and to All Priests of the Church 25¢ — EP0688

On the Mercy of God (Dives in Misericordia) 50¢ — EP0863

On the Mystery and Worship of the Eucharist (Dominicae Cenae) 35¢ — EP0895

The Redeemer of Man (Redemptor hominis) 50¢ — EP0978

Redemptor Hominis (Polish) 50¢ — EP0979

On Human Work (Laborem exercens) 60¢ — EP0862

The above may be ordered from any of the addresses at the end of this volume.

Daughters of St. Paul

IN MASSACHUSETTS
50 St. Paul's Ave., Jamaica Plain, Boston, MA 02130;
617-522-8911; 617-522-0875.
172 Tremont Street, Boston, MA 02111; **617-426-5464;
617-426-4230.**

IN NEW YORK
78 Fort Place, Staten Island, NY 10301; **212-447-5071; 212-447-5086.**
59 East 43rd Street, New York, NY 10017; **212-986-7580.**
625 East 187th Street, Bronx, NY 10458; **212-584-0440.**
525 Main Street, Buffalo, NY 14203; **716-847-6044.**

IN NEW JERSEY
Hudson Mall — Route 440 and Communipaw Ave.,
Jersey City, NJ 07304; **201-433-7740.**

IN CONNECTICUT
202 Fairfield Ave., Bridgeport, CT 06604; **203-335-9913.**

IN OHIO
2105 Ontario Street (at Prospect Ave.), Cleveland, OH 44115;
216-621-9427.
25 E. Eighth Street, Cincinnati, OH 45202; **513-721-4838;
513-421-5733.**

IN PENNSYLVANIA
1719 Chestnut Street, Philadelphia, PA 19103; **215-568-2638.**

IN VIRGINIA
1025 King Street, Alexandria, VA 22314; **703-683-1741;
703-549-3806.**

IN FLORIDA
2700 Biscayne Blvd., Miami, FL 33137; **305-573-1618.**

IN LOUISIANA
4403 Veterans Memorial Blvd., Metairie, LA 70002; **504-887-7631;
504-887-0113.**
1800 South Acadian Thruway, P.O. Box 2028, Baton Rouge, LA 70821;
504-343-4057; 504-381-9485.

IN MISSOURI
1001 Pine Street (at North 10th), St. Louis, MO 63101; **314-621-0346;
314-231-1034.**

IN ILLINOIS
172 North Michigan Ave., Chicago, IL 60601; **312-346-4228;
312-346-3240.**

IN TEXAS
114 Main Plaza, San Antonio, TX 78205; **512-224-8101.**

IN CALIFORNIA
1570 Fifth Ave., San Diego, CA 92101; **619-232-1442.**
46 Geary Street, San Francisco, CA 94108; **415-781-5180.**

IN HAWAII
1143 Bishop Street, Honolulu, HI 96813; **808-521-2731.**

IN ALASKA
750 West 5th Ave., Anchorage, AK 99501; **907-272-8183.**

IN CANADA
3022 Dufferin Street, Toronto 395, Ontario, Canada.

IN ENGLAND
128, Notting Hill Gate, London W11 3QG, England.
133 Corporation Street, Birmingham B4 6PH, England.
5A-7 Royal Exchange Square, Glasgow G1 3AH, England.
82 Bold Street, Liverpool L1 4HR, England.

IN AUSTRALIA
58 Abbotsford Rd., Homebush, N.S.W. 2140, Australia